# Exploring Antarctica

Written by Shalini Vallepur
Designed by Jasmine Pointer

©This edition published in 2023. First published in 2022.
BookLife Publishing Ltd.
King's Lynn, Norfolk, PE30 4LS, UK

ISBN 978-1-80155-158-8

All rights reserved. Printed in China.
A catalogue record for this book is available
from the British Library.

Exploring Antarctica
Written by Shalini Vallepur. Adapted by William Anthony
Designed by Jasmine Pointer

FSC
www.fsc.org
MIX
Paper from
responsible sources
FSC® C113515

# An Introduction to Accessible Readers...

Our 'really readable' Accessible Readers have been specifically created to support the reading development of young readers with learning differences, such as dyslexia.

Our aim is to share our love of books with children, providing the same learning and developmental opportunities to every child.

**INCREASED FONT SIZE AND SPACING** improves readability and ensures text feels much less crowded.

**OFF-WHITE BACKGROUNDS ON MATTE PAPER** improves text contrast and avoids dazzling readers.

**SIMPLIFIED PAGE LAYOUT** reduces distractions and aids concentration.

**CAREFULLY CRAFTED** along guidelines set out in the British Dyslexia Association's Dyslexia-Friendly Style Guide.

Images courtesy of Shutterstock.com. Cover – Mara008, Kotomiti Okuna, TerraceStudio, Volodymyr Goinyk. 4–5 – NicoElNino, _Pyty. 6–7 – Harvepino, 2j architecture. 8–9 – Johnna Goodyear, Matt Makes Photos. 10–11 – Armin Rose, polarman. 12–13 – Fotos593, MU YEE TING. 14–15 – vladsilver, Willyam Bradberry. 16–17 – Tory Kallman, reisegraf. ch. 18–19 – Ken Griffiths, Liam Quinn, CC BY-SA 2.0 <https://creativecommons.org/licenses/by-sa/2.0>, via Wikimedia Commons, Tarpan. 20–21 – U. Schzeibach (U. ▢▢▢▢▢▢▢), circa 1835, Public domain, via Wikimedia Commons, no credit, Public domain, via Wikimedia Commons. 22–23 – chanasorn jele, Tatiana Grozetskaya. 24–25 – fivepointsix, demamiel62. 26–27 – Susan Santa Maria, geniusksy. 28–29 – LeManna, Scharfsinn.

# Contents

Page 4   What Is a Continent?

Page 6   Antarctica

Page 8   Weather

Page 10  Living in Antarctica

Page 12  Aurora Australis

Page 14  Animals

Page 18  Plants

Page 20  Exploring

Page 22  Climate Change

Page 24  Sea Levels

Page 26  Helping Antarctica

Page 30  Index

Page 31  Antarctica: Quiz

# What Is a Continent?

A continent is a very large bit of land. There are seven continents on Earth. They are Africa, Antarctica, Asia, Australia, Europe, North America and South America. All of the continents are split up into countries, except Antarctica.

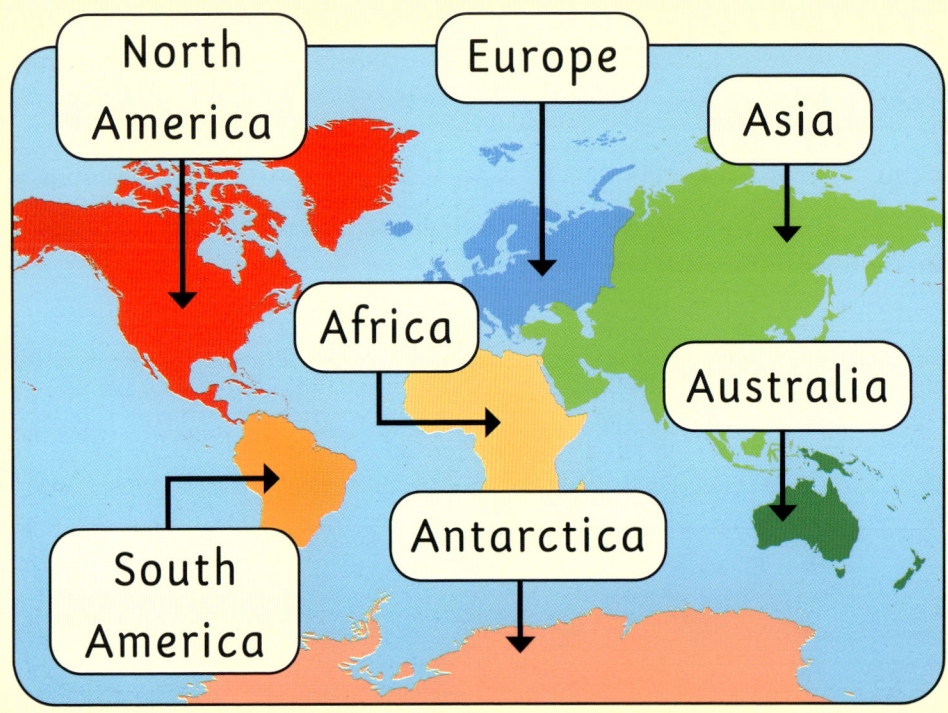

There are people living on each one of the seven continents. Asia is the continent with the most people living there. Antarctica is the continent with the fewest people living there. Each continent has different types of weather, landscape and ways of life.

# Antarctica

Antarctica is the continent that is farthest south. It does not have any countries. It is split into lots of different parts called territories. Each of the territories is owned by different countries around the world.

Nobody lives in Antarctica forever because it is so difficult to survive there. Scientists and workers usually live in research stations for just a short time to learn about Antarctica. People sometimes visit Antarctica just to see what it is like there.

# Weather

The Equator is an imaginary line that runs around the middle of Earth. Places that are far away from the Equator are usually colder than places that are close to it. Antarctica is one of the farthest places from the Equator, which means it is one of the coldest.

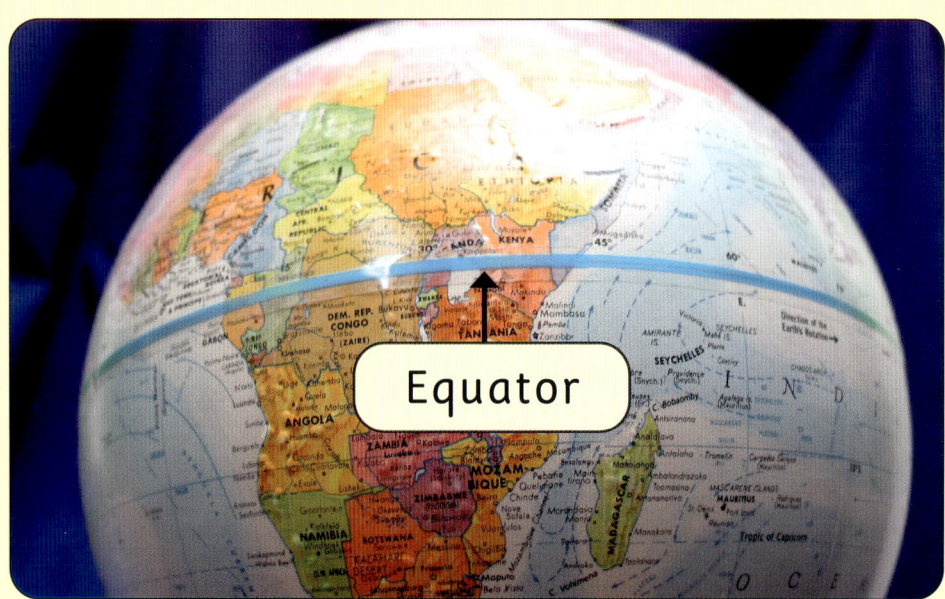

Antarctica is very cold and there is a lot of wind. Most of the continent is completely covered in snow and ice all year round. Antarctica is called a polar desert because there is not much rain at all.

# Living in Antarctica

The scientists who live in Antarctica study its weather, animals, plants and rocks. They have to make sure they are dressed properly and keep warm. Many people wear goggles to stop their eyes freezing shut!

It can be very difficult to live in Antarctica. Polar night happens during winter. This is when there is usually no sunlight for around 30 days.

# Aurora Australis

The aurora australis can be seen during polar night. It is sometimes called the southern lights. They are natural, swirling lights in the sky that light up the dark night in lots of different patterns and colours.

The aurora australis is not the only one of its kind. The arctic circle is the coldest region at the top of the planet. Here, you can see the aurora borealis, which we also call the northern lights.

# Animals

The animals that live in Antarctica have special body parts that help them to live in the cold weather.

Emperor penguins have strong claws on their feet. These help them to walk in deep snow and on slippery ice.

Killer whales live in the waters around Antarctica. They have a thick layer of blubber under their skin that helps to keep them warm. Killer whales are sometimes called orcas. Killer whales usually hunt for food in groups called pods.

Albatrosses have very large wings. In fact, they have the longest wings of any bird on the planet! These wings help them to fly a long way to look for food, which is helpful when there is not much food around.

Seals have large eyes that help them to see under water. Having better sight under water makes it easier for the seals to catch other animals for food. Seals also have blubber under their skin that helps keep them warm.

# Plants

Not many plants can grow in Antarctica because of the harsh weather. Plants that do grow there have special parts that help them to survive.

Antarctic hair grass has long roots that help it stay in place when it is windy.

Antarctic pearlwort grows near the coast where there is more water. Pearlwort flowers grow in the summer months.

On the islands around Antarctica, plant-like moss grows on rocks. Penguins sometimes build nests using moss that they find.

# Exploring

Many people have tried to explore Antarctica. The weather makes these trips very difficult. Many explorers had to leave Antarctica early because of bad weather.

Fabian Gottlieb von Bellingshausen was one of the first explorers to see land in the Antarctic Circle.

In 1911, Roald Amundsen became the first person to reach the South Pole. The trip was very dangerous. It took two months for his group to reach their goal.

# Climate Change

Climate change is when the normal weather of a place changes over a long amount of time. When the temperature of the entire planet starts to get warmer, we call it global warming.

Climate change and global warming are caused by lots of the things that humans do. It can be caused by the way we make electricity and even the ways that we travel.

## Sea Levels

Antarctica is getting warmer because of climate change. This has caused some of the ice around Antarctica to start melting. Melting ice and snow from Antarctica is starting to make the sea levels around the world get higher.

This can cause floods in other places around the world.

Some animals that rely on snow and ice to survive could even end up losing their homes because of climate change.

# Helping Antarctica

There are lots of things that we can do to slow down climate change.

Things powered by coal, oil and gas are big causes of climate change. If we can avoid some of these things, we can help our planet.

Lots of the ways that we make electricity are bad for the planet. These include burning coal, oil and gas. If we use things such as sunlight, wind or the ocean to make electricity instead, we can slow down climate change.

Many cars, buses, planes and motorcycles are powered by engines that use oil as well. Instead of taking the car to school, why not walk or cycle instead? That way, we get good exercise and help the planet!

We could also use cars powered by electricity instead of oil. If we also use electricity that has been made using sunlight or the wind, then we are helping our planet even more!

# Index:

auroras 12–13

climate change 22–27

continents 4–6, 9

Equator 8

people 5, 7, 10, 20–21, 23

sea levels 24–25

South Pole 21

weather 5, 8–10, 18, 20, 22

# Antarctica: Quiz

1. What are some of the reasons that it is difficult for living things to survive in Antarctica?

2. How does climate change affect the ice and snow in Antarctica?

3. What are some of the things we can do to slow climate change?

4. Which aurora do we see in Antarctica: the aurora borealis or the aurora australis?

5. If you were a scientist, what would you most like to study in Antarctica?

# Helpful Hints for Reading at Home

This 'really readable' Accessible Reader has been carefully written and designed to help children with learning differences whether they are reading in the classroom or at home. However, there are some extra ways in which you can help your child at home.

- Try to provide a quiet space for your child to read, with as few distractions as possible.

- Try to allow your child as much time as they need to decode the letters and words on the page.

- Reading with a learning difference can be frustrating and difficult. Try to let your child take short, managed breaks between reading sessions if they begin to feel frustrated.

- Build your child's confidence with positive praise and encouragement throughout.

- Your child's teacher, as well as many charities, can provide you with lots of tips and techniques to help your child read at home.